For Mary Ann,

Bless you for your interest and your support. I was watching you, because your expression was so earnest and absorbed.

A Child Of The King

by

Patricia Klinger Schrope

Patricia Schrope

Bloomington, IN

authorHOUSE®

Milton Keynes, UK

AuthorHouse™
1663 Liberty Drive, Suite 200
Bloomington, IN 47403
www.authorhouse.com
Phone: 1-800-839-8640

AuthorHouse™ UK Ltd.
500 Avebury Boulevard
Central Milton Keynes, MK9 2BE
www.authorhouse.co.uk
Phone: 08001974150

First published by AuthorHouse 4/30/2007

ISBN: 978-1-4343-0513-8 (sc)

Library of Congress Control Number: 2007902490

Printed in the United States of America
Bloomington, Indiana

This book is printed on acid-free paper.

Dedication: To the family of love that got us through it.

To my daughter, AUDREY MELISSA. I wrote every word primarily for you. I was afraid that you might forget some of your big sister. But, every day I learn more and still more that you caught and kept in your heart. Pain and loss were certainly there for you, although they never diminished your incandescent and voluminous smile that warms and cheers us all. I love you, my Sunshine.

To my daughter, KATIE REBECCA, who is a dear sister to Tracy even though you never met. Thank you for never tiring of stories and photographs of Tracy. Your sweetness still serves as a healing balm to Audrey and me. We wished and prayed for your arrival. We got just what we wanted. We love you.

To EUGENE SCHROPE, my husband, for your devotion and kindness through this writing. You met Tracy when she was sitting in her playpen. Your letter was one of the first expressions of solace I received. Always supportive in my years of grief, you often cried with me. Thank you for adorning Tracy's grave with mostly purple flowers so often and so willingly. I love you for commissioning a portrait of Tracy to keep her likeness available every day.

To JIM C. COUCH, Physician extraordinaire. You saved Tracy so many times and ultimately allowed us to keep her for four years full of cherished days. We could trust you with every diagnosis and with every direction you gave. You sang Audrey love songs as you drove her to Oklahoma City to see me. You made her feel safe. Often, you called my eldest, Tracy Couch. That endeared you to us. You have to love and trust a doctor like that.

To La RITA COUCH, for giving Audrey your love. You were a stand-in Mom whenever it was necessary. You gave us food, shelter and wise counsel. Always cheerful and loving, we call each other cousins, and I count you as my very dearest friend. You can't beat that!

Acknowledgements

JEFFREY PINCUS, Ph.D., for encouraging me to publish this book. He knew that this was a heartfelt desire of mine, and he helped me to realize that now was the time. Always gentle and intellectual, we read excerpts aloud to each other, and I treasure that.

CONNIE WEHRY, my technical whiz who transferred my typed pages to the computer. She was steadfast and dependable and compassionately touched by the content. I have acquired a new friend.

Prologue

A parchment card in front of me reads, "Date of Death, July 28. Age, 10 years, 6 months, 18 days." I open the pages of your adventure in this way only to prepare the reader for what is to come. I find myself trusting that you will forgive me. My experience with adults reveals, with few exceptions, that "they" cannot easily accept your problem and its ultimate outcome with the same grace, dignity and tenacity that you, a child, could. More than anything, my wish is for these words to be a loving tribute to you. This is neither an inspired message of victory over grief, nor is it a picture of a mother of great strength, because, in fact, I am still living with a deep sadness. I struggle and flounder just as any mother would do. I want desperately to share your story to cheerfully applaud the stoic, smiling soldier, Tracy Elizabeth. If others obtain just a fragment of strength and acceptance in their struggles, my work will be worthwhile. My position is quite apostolic. I will be the instrument utilized to proclaim a kind of Good News about your precious life. Let me be your messenger. Let me demonstrate still another time the way that children so often, and very ably, may lead their elders. All we need to do is to step back and observe the miraculous inborn knowledge that the young have often revealed throughout the ages! You've had this knowledge all along, and have been gracious enough not to flaunt it in our faces! How polite of you. Was the joyous deception almost too much to contain?

Chapter 1: Celestial Dance

The wonder of a new life born for me to carefully nourish, love and teach began early in the morning and fittingly early in the New Year. Good Samaritan Hospital in Pottsville, Pennsylvania, provided your initial needs. I will never forget how the Catholic sisters in attendance nicknamed you "Little Saint Joseph." Odd, I thought, since you were a lovely image of femininity even dressed in a plain diaper and shirt ensemble! The sisters told me several days later that they fondly called you Joseph because of a certain saintly expression on your face, and because of the way that nature patterned both your coiffures. I let them have their fantasies, but I don't mind telling the rest of the world that I always thought a Saint in the female gender would have been infinitely more like it! In any event you were magnificently gorgeous, winsome, totally healthy, and ready to conquer the beasts!

It appeared that there were not going to be too many foes to overcome in Pennsylvania. One smile from you, and the people within your realm were puppets to do as you desired. I suppose that this was to be expected, the first child born to your adoring parents, as well as being the first grandchild. Even those who had not yet met you fell under the spell of happiness. There was a sweet letter addressed to you by my aunt when you were just two weeks old that said what was in all our hearts: "The whole family tree

1

is blooming with pride!" I kept that letter in your baby book for you to enjoy someday.

Your daddy had chosen the military as his career. I now can see that it enabled you to experience much more of the United States than many of your peers. Let's be thankful for your many homes in various states. This was one opportunity that helped you to live life with real enthusiasm and more maturity than would be true of most children. We lived a very short while in California, just long enough to have you receive the Sacrament of Baptism. Then, on to North Dakota!

Here is where your spirited personality really flourished. "Boy-dee-lee-low"* was what you would exclaim in your baby language. You squealed it when I would come into your bedroom in the morning. You shouted it while you were being bathed in the kitchen sink. You seemed to be expressing joy and delight. "Boy-dee-lee-low, right back at you," as I tried to imitate your wondrous expression. Then there was your Penow?** He was a light brown classic teddy bear with a music box inside a zipper. Penow and you were inseparable and you named him all by yourself. I was a good Mommy who laundered your stuffed animals often. In order to do that with your guarded consent, you stayed in a little chair and watched Penow as he swam in the washing machine. Then, quite impatiently, you waited while the poor dear bear was drying. All of this took place in our drab basement, but you were on a mission. On another occasion we took a flight somewhere, and in deplaning we left the Penow sitting in your seat. Well, the myriad of tears you shed and the wails emanating from your body rendered the airport staff so defenseless that they delayed the next flight just a matter of minutes before returning the little bear to your loving arms. (More than a decade later I discovered

---

* boidelelo - cosmic or celestial dance, melody that each of us is dimly aware of, from this side to the other side.

** penow - look at him (her), light brown mare.

that your baby language just may have been a universal tongue of some sort. Check footnote.)

It was your nap time, and I had carried you to bed about three times, each time more vigorously insisting that two year old girls needed a midday snooze, and that I was certainly not above a little tap on the bottom. Well, on your fourth trip downstairs, I obliged with said punishment. To my shock, you trembled and became crimson with anger. And, next followed a spell that was to hang over my head for years to come. With pointed finger, you solemnly decreed, "YOU SHALL HAVE NO PIE!!!" Never were death penalties or four letter words so plainly enunciated.

You progressed beautifully in every way, opening the way for quiet boastfulness on the part of your Mommy. In retrospect, I am nearly sure that you matured so nicely in order to become a "big sister" in the best sense of the word to Audrey Melissa, just two years your junior. You were separate blessings to me. Audrey will endlessly sing your praises, and I am so pleased that the two of you were never rivals.

One Christmas when you were very small and even more precocious, you demonstrated to your Mommy and Daddy that Santa could save his time on gift wrapping. Santa's helpers had been very busy attending to details on Christmas Eve. There were the dutiful things to assemble, things to wrap and to display. It was probably three in the morning before we laid down for a short winter's nap. You appeared by our bed early in the morning and said, "Santa came and he brought me a little piano."

We sort of smiled and thought, perhaps it was wishful thinking on your part. Then, you said, "Audrey got a monkey with a banana." We sat bolt upright when you continued, "Mommy got purple earrings and Daddy got a robe," and so on. That was the Christmas we missed, because you had tiptoed all alone downstairs, quietly opened all the presents, and displayed them under the tree. We couldn't be upset with you . . . not when you even threw away all the used ribbons and paper! It was those four hours of sleep we wished we'd found under the tree. It's a universal dilemma for elves, I suppose.

T-R-A-C-Y, that is how you mastered printing your very own name at a mere four years of age. We broke in a giant chalk board, which would be hung on the kitchen wall wherever we made our home, even before the mundane kitchen utensils, pots and pans found their niche. My little ladies continued to delight everyone they knew. By this time you wanted your own bedrooms, the privacy of your own closets, and a place for your own toys. Granted. Ah! But there was a catch. You both had every intention of continuing to sleep together! And, so it was. Daddy and I saw no harm in this special closeness, secretly we were proud as peacocks. About this same time, I began to endearingly call Audrey my little sunshine. She radiated beams of happiness then, and as a big girl now, goes right on with her infectious grin and laughter. I want you to know how firmly I believe that you molded her into the sweet, uncomplicated child that she is. A while after you both had been tucked in for the night it was my habit to go back into your bedroom to see if you were covered and asleep. More often than not, Audrey was already in the land of nod when my eyes fell on the same tender scene. You would be gently stroking your sister's hair, and simultaneously rubbing her "baby soft hands." Do you remember doing that? You told me that was the best way to put yourself to sleep.

One lovely afternoon Audrey was catching her siesta in the playpen while you and I sat on our back porch. The day was perfect, somewhere between the frigid sub zero temperatures and the sultry locusts. We were in Minot, North Dakota, so anything was possible weather-wise. You were studying our dog and our neighbors' dog when you mused, "Have you ever noticed that Frizzle's belly and Schatzie's belly are different?" "Yes," I said, hoping that would suffice because I noticed that you were not referring to bellies. Oh, no, you were checking out the male and female anatomies which indeed were different. "Why is that?" you continued. I knew that I had to catch a breath before I got into sex education with my inquisitive daughter. I went into the safe area of the kitchen, poured a cup of coffee then rejoined you on the porch. "Now, about the dogs' bellies," I began. "Oh, I already figured that out, Mommy. I figured that dachshunds come with, and wire haired fox terriers come without." "Exactly," I agreed. And I thought I had to teach you!

Disney movies, books and such constantly bring back to me favorite yarns to spin about your very young childhood. In the film immortalizing Bambi we comprehend events from the animals' point of view. All the wild beasts chill when they murmur of "the hunters." They are no less feared than fires or earthquakes. It had not become apparent that you did not equate man with hunter until one fateful day when a neighbor came to invite your Dad to join him in that sport. You pressed him to explain just what hunters do. The neighbor enlightened you in a boastful sportsman's way, and to his amusement you were amply horrified. Later in the same week our tarnished neighbor made a return visit, this time carrying a large brown bag. In actuality he had but assisted his wife with grocery shopping and had requested some big, hard bones from the butcher. The bones were for our respective pet dogs, but when you pleaded repeatedly to know the contents of the brown bag, he couldn't resist a slightly mean joke on you. Your former friend opened his bounty and boomed, "JUST SOME BAMBI BONES, TRACY." The hunter was roundly ignored by you for a long, long time.

Our tour of duty was over in North Dakota. The family needed a rest, so we played a little in the vacation spots of Minnesota. While there, we visited a large pottery factory. The factory was downstairs, and a very casual lunchroom overlooked the shoppers below. Audrey was the picture of decorum in her high chair, contentedly munching on french fries and other finger foods. I glanced at you and saw your excitement building when you witnessed three Catholic sisters checking the wares below us. You shrieked gleefully, "Oh, look at the Jesus Christ ladies." and "I want to see the Jesus Christ ladies!" You were very loud and quite persistent. I was mildly mortified . . . enough that I excused myself from lunch and went downstairs to apologize to the three humble sisters (right out of the *Sound of Music*). I made my apologies, and said that my little girl meant no disrespect, but that she saw those bright, shiny crosses and became loudly exuberant. "Oh, no disrespect taken," the eldest sister assured me. "What did she say, did she think we were witches?" Realizing then that the sisters never even heard you, I said, "No, she called you the Jesus Christ ladies." All the sisters giggled timidly and the eldest offered, "That's probably the loveliest name we were ever called." Your dad was typically uncomfortable with any outward shows of emotion. We made a somewhat hasty exit. Then on to the grandeur of Niagara Falls. I was struck with the idea that if my boisterous one had other loud exclamations to be blurted out, she wouldn't be heard over the roar of the falls!

We shared the grandchildren in Pennsylvania, then all of us drove to our favorite place in the world, Ocean City, New Jersey! How you breathed in all the pleasure that was to be derived from the sand, the BIG ocean, the boardwalk, the bicycle rides in the mornings. The ocean mesmerized you, as it had me all my life. We both whispered like double agents something to the effect that if we could just divert the attention of the lifeguards away from ourselves, we undoubtedly could walk, swim and float to England. Once there, we could visit the Queen, and return unnoticed just as we had departed! Oh, Honey, you made me as young as you. With our imaginations leading us we only had to follow the leader and home base could be England or Oz!

We did return one more time to our old friend the sea, but it was not the same. I have real photographs and mental pictures of that last complete family trip to the sandy beaches of Ocean City. You were easily exhausted due to medical treatment. That famous boardwalk proved to be a cruel test of your endurance to the sun's sweltering heat and to walks that must have been like senseless marathons to your aching legs. Your dad carried you much of the time. We knew how sick you had become, so it was understandable for us to hope that you could enjoy that vacation. I am sorry that it was impossible. It was just one of those wishes that did not come true.

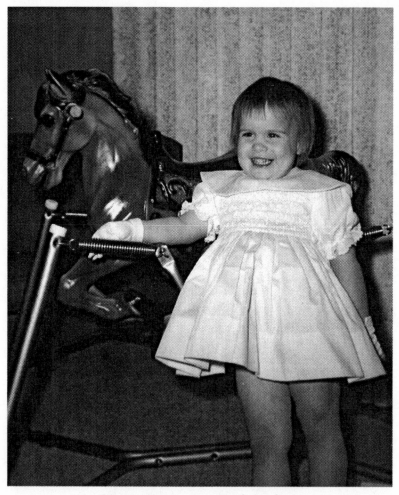

Tracy, Easter in North Dakota

Birth announcement, the whole family tree was blooming with pride

Tracy at 16 months, model for a Spring fashion show in North Dakota

20 month old Tracy with Mommy
in western Pennsylvania

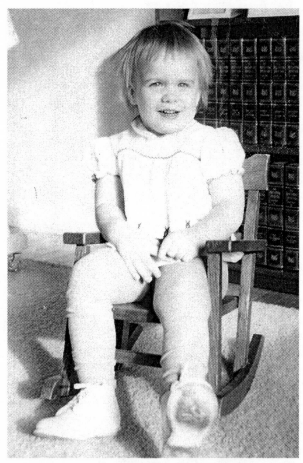

*Tracy at 2 years in Great-grandfather's
hand made rocking chair*

Chapter 2: *Storm Warnings*

We had just moved to Oklahoma. The summer was nearly over, and we were preparing you for kindergarten. Your Mommy may be wrong, but I surmise that this was to be your most vividly recalled fun-time. Your teacher was excellent, and your days were prime. Little Audrey was attending nursery school, busily adding words to her vocabulary like "hibernate" and "metamorphosis." Sixty-four dollar words like those became her weapons against any of the older and taller kids who wrongly thought that she could not play at their levels. Again I must compliment you because you adopted a love me, love my sister attitude. You truly were your sister's keeper . . . And we all adore you for that. Upon the completion of kindergarten, the summer was very relaxed and uneventful.

On to first grade. Yea! The first day of school! One night early in September the family attended our first authentic rodeo in western Oklahoma. You girls were allowed to stay up late on a school night for the occasion. This was why you came home from school so tired the next day, I reasoned. I thought a bit more of it when the following day your lethargy returned. I expressed my concern to neighbors who momentarily dispelled my uneasiness by telling me that their children always came home tired from first grade. One friend of mine suggested that it was probably just the transition from kindergarten (half day) to regular school hours.

Audrey was trying to get over a case of tonsillitis, and would be making a return visit to our family doctor, the one with the giant shoes! I called your teacher to see about having you excused early so that you might have a good physical examination. She agreed.

The ride from our house to the doctor's office in Cordell consumes only about twenty minutes. With not too much scenic distraction, the ride itself prompts conversation. We did not have a morose chat, but rather a serious one, I thought, since my oldest companion was only six. You and Audrey somehow became inquisitive that afternoon about what makes people die? I replied without hesitation, that apart from accidents and old age, heart attacks, cancer and strokes probably were the causes. Both my passengers agreed, since reports of deaths via the television or the newspapers had these same culprits named as the cause. I reminded us all that we were only concerned with tonsils and routine physicals that afternoon.

Your little sister said a jubilant, germ-free "ah-h-h" to the wooden tongue depressor, and now it was your turn to meet the physician. Nature and Mom's good cooking worked hand in hand to make your little body chunky and a bit rounded out. Never could any discerning person say that you were fat. Let it suffice to say that you more resembled a budding football star than an Anna Pavlova. I had little to supply in the medical history department, due to the fact that chicken pox was the only illness ever to visit you. The doctor asked if there were any symptoms that urged me to bring you to his office. I told him about your unnatural fatigue following a school day, and of a puzzling low grade temperature. So low, in fact, that the elevation was not great enough to warrant aspirin. Next, there followed a tactless remark by the one with the giant shoes. (I thought his foot belonged in his mouth!) "Tracy," he said, "you have a very big tummy." How to win friends and influence people, I thought, nearly aloud! After regaining my composure, you probably recall how Mommy came to your defense in stating that the tummy to which he was

14

referring was, in actuality, your diaphragm and that if he found it to be somewhat enlarged, it had to be because you were going to be a world famous opera singer.

Tracy with Grandma's geraniums in Pennsylvania

Tracy, age 6 in western Oklahoma,
three months before chaos.

Chapter 3: Chaos

The scene changed. It remains a question to me how you two were literally whisked away, and I was ushered into the doctor's office with the door closed behind me. He leaned way across his desk, spoke precisely, yet scarcely above a whisper and proceeded to tell me that Tracy Elizabeth was a terribly sick child. I said nothing. He went on to say that you had a potentially fatal disease. I said nothing. It was a malignancy, to be sure, but further tests would confirm it in the morning. Still I remained mute. I believed this man and his diagnosis. Can one be too overwhelmingly frightened to cry? The wretched disease is known to a small number of distraught parents as Wilm's Tumor. Mercifully, it is a rarity. Guardian angels piloted us home late that afternoon. They must have, since I had no awareness of steering or accelerating! My brain was repeating Wilm's Tumor, potentially fatal disease, malignancy, Wilm's Tumor!!! My back seat passengers amused themselves by alternately singing, deciding what game to play, and happily sighing that they could once again be bed-buddies since Audrey's tonsillitis had been whipped.

I arranged for a sitter to watch you girls while I met with your daddy to tell him how my day had been . . . impossible for me to keep this knowledge to myself during the endless waking hours of your day. Daddy simply didn't react. I wondered if he didn't believe any of the horror story? Yes, later I knew that he had. What more could he say to me than I had said to the one who made your diagnosis? We agreed to take you in the morning together, for the x-rays that would confirm or deny any such devastating illness. I cannot speak for your father, but as far as I was concerned, the x-rays would only serve to support the surgeon. I needed no more confirmation. Do these statements sound pessimistic or like words that a person without faith might utter? I truly hope that is not the picture I am presenting. It was a kind of resignation to the ugly reality that I so painfully was experiencing. The night was long, dear, and my eyes remained moist and opened.

Saturday morning came, the tests were done, and arrangements made to enter Presbyterian Hospital in Oklahoma City for emergency surgery the following morning. The blue Grand Prix was destined to become a more comfortable style ambulance in the days ahead. Our bags were packed. Dr. Jim said, "What do you plan to do with Audrey?" "Take her along, of course," I answered. I reminded him that we were a military family, that our relatives were in Pennsylvania, and that I hardly knew anyone on base that would look after our daughter, largely because we were quite new there. Dr. Couch said that he and his wife had anticipated all my responses. He said, "You don't know what you'll be up against in the city, and you won't be able to take care of Audrey or to take her into the hospital." He pushed on very quickly to say that his wife would keep Audrey. He said that she wouldn't lack for playmates or for love and good home cooking. My next recollection is that of taking my youngest daughter, just four years old, hand in hand to their porch. I knocked on the door, introduced us to Mrs. Couch and gave Audrey somewhat willingly, but dazed, to her care. Audrey clutched a small green floral suitcase and her Puddin' doll. One of my dolls was left behind with a stranger. I trusted Dr. Jim's directives as much as I did his diagnosis. I didn't know then how wonderful his wife was. Our meeting proved providential, but I had learned in the last two days how to weep internally, silently so that no one would notice.

Presbyterian Hospital was a two hour drive from our house. How many times we were destined to make that trip! Since Wilm's originates in the kidney, and your involvement was most extensive, a right nephrectomy (removal of the kidney) was done. The operation was a tedious one . . . Not entirely a success because a threatening amount of malignancy was inoperable due to the location.

My next several recollections are not easy to assemble. There was your surgeon with his news, the pathologist's report, my phone call to your grandparents who knew the awful outcome by their daughter's incoherence and inability to speak, even though I had dialed their number mechanically. By far the harshest, most cruel sounds, were different voices all with the same story to repeat; "She is too old to survive." "We have some cures with children not as old as Tracy." The pediatrician, insensitively and with definite assuredness said (and I overheard), "I wouldn't give a plugged nickel for her chances" . . . Too old, they said! Can anyone fathom a girl of six too old for anything? Why, you still played with dolls; I did not allow you to cross a street without supervision; you knew there was a Santa; you only recently learned such feats as tying bows or mastering a two-wheeled bike. Still, the learned voices said that you were too old!

Finally, I was allowed to see you in the intensive care unit five minutes out of every hour. Not a line of your account will be exaggerated, I swear. What I saw that time was never to be forgotten. My daughter was so much closer to the spiritual side of life than the physical. You were not pale, but gray. Had you ever been healthy and radiant even one day in your life? It was hard to remember. One of the nurses in charge came out for me before the hour was spent. She did not want to upset you, but it was time to give you an injection for pain and sedation. When I entered your room, you said that you didn't want a shot. You mustered up enough strength to add that you didn't NEED a shot for sleep, if I would please sing you to sleep. You even had the requested number on your lips, something that I had sung to you every night of your earliest childhood. Darling, I took your cool hand under the oxygen tent, and began the most meaningful and difficult labor of love that I had ever been asked to demonstrate. It is quite a sensation to sing under tension loud enough to be audible under a churning, grinding oxygen tent, and, at the same time soft enough to provide a lullaby without disturbing several adult patients in the surrounding beds.

Loo, loo, loo loo loo . . . Hushabye
Dream of the angels way up high
Loo, loo, loo loo loo . . . Don't you cry
Momma won't go away.
Sleep in my arms while you still can
Childhood is but a day . . .
Even when you're a great big girl
Momma won't go away.*

You needed to hear it over and over again, sometimes a little louder. I sang it for you, just as you wished. And then, Tracy Elizabeth went to sleep peacefully . . . No nasty shots!

---

* Hushabye by Sammy Fain, Jerry Seelen and Danny Thomas

Audrey, age 4, sleeping with Puddin' doll.
Photo by J.C. Couch

Chapter 4: The Plan

The staff involved in your case visibly exuded amazement. A super recovery was in progress right before their wondering eyes. There was to be as much radiation therapy as your small frame could tolerate without damage. And, chemotherapy (administered intravenously) was begun before any of us could catch our breaths. The three-fold treatment plan for you might well have been labeled Highly Explosive. Medical experts preferred to call it, aggressive. A word about the surgeon who did the nephrectomy. You and I will forever be exalting that man. On a very few occasions, Tracy, your morale dropped. One such time, in an effort to boost you, I heartily agreed that the road behind had been, at best, difficult. I prodded to see if you had harbored any pleasant thoughts along that road. Without the least hesitation, you spoke fondly of Dr. Miller who looked surprisingly like grandpa, you thought, and he was the sweetest alarm clock ever! So it was that I learned how he took time first thing every morning, even when you were nearly well, to drive across town . . . to wake you with a kiss and begin your day with, "Good morning, Beautiful!"

Back again to join the host of first grade friends. In some subjects you were ahead of the class. How can that be possible? Call it perseverance or go-power, but, where you are concerned, many "believe it or not" situations occurred. During your course of radiation the issue at hand for my daughter was how not to be behind in her studies. I was able to secure a tutor for you, and did you work like a Trojan! You weren't the type to let a bothersome thing like vomiting interfere with modern math or earning a certificate for library achievement. You and I decided together that the "sick girl" image wasn't for you. The lump was out of your tummy, and now you could skip rope and play hop scotch with the best of 'em!

How well I recall a telephone conversation with a very important pediatrician in our lives from Presbyterian Hospital. It was nearly Thanksgiving, and I required some objective person to tell me if I had anything at all for which to be thankful in that year. I could almost smell his pipe long distance as he pondered over what to reply. He suggested I count the number of days that had passed since September tenth and thank God for each of them. It was his gentle method of reminding me that your prognosis was somewhat dim. I had barely returned the telephone receiver to its proper place before deciding mentally what my course would entail. I was going to relate to you as a loving mother making no distinction whatever between you and Audrey. You, above all else, had become a challenge for me to guide and to guard. You were never to be denied a normal childhood. Normality included picnics, swimming, school-work. Also, it included discipline. I cherished you too much to allow you special privileges that would ruin your unspoiled personality. One more requirement in the course ahead of me: Hereafter, if there had to be recurrences of the original Wilm's Tumor, words like tumor, malignancy, cancer, radiation had to be verboten in your presence! The patient was a child, my child. You could understand, without fear, substitutions like lump, growth, x-ray treatment, and serious problem. I was determined on this subject. Whether the medical profession as a whole disagreed with me, made not a hair of difference. Those doctors who so ably and compassionately attended you complied with my wishes. In my prayers I constantly asked God to reward all of your medical geniuses, and especially the one who originally discovered your problem. Jim C. Couch, M.D., cannot forever

their day. That silly dog always seemed to relish and revel in the occasion. Isn't that right?

Nearly a whole year has gone by since we first heard about Wilm's. Second grade is in full swing. And, I had corresponded with numerous friends about the delighted mood I am put into each morning when I watch both daughters gleefully chattering as they trot off to school. Some of these friends were very much aware that to begin one more year of school was, indeed some kind of miracle. It certainly had not been guaranteed or taken for granted. The Tuesday appointments for your medicine had not been changed. We were nearing the end of the conventional period of time prescribed for chemotherapy. So, it was expected that all concerned would be in festive, celebrating spirits the day of your last shot of periwinkle juice. All during this time, the assistants and technicians had been consistently efficient, with a dash of special interest. They congratulated you for being such a good patient, so cooperative and mature. (In the back of their minds they undoubtedly swelled with pride that you were alive.) As a joint effort, they presented Audrey with a mock certificate they had carefully made, citing her "Perfect Attendance." Doctor Jim told us to make the two-hour trip east in one month for a thorough examination and diagnostic x-rays, proof of your continued well-being. We agreed. It was then that I confided what I had been thinking for quite some time. I told him that it was no accident that his initials were J.C. (Figure that one out, you students of theology!) Later it was revealed to me that the youths of the community referred to J.C. as Johnny Cool... Ho!... I prefer my analogy!

If I were reading this, my maternal instincts would eventually question where did Audrey keep her young self during her sister's frequent trials? Well, she didn't keep herself. The Couch family repeatedly embraced her as one of their brood. La Rita Couch was my stand-in on numerous occasions. I had a feeling it was no accident that she resembled my sister in an uncanny way.

The month went by uneventfully except for Halloween. That year, you girls carved your own pumpkins. One was funny, and one was positively ghoulish. After the carving was done, Mommy made her annual pumpkin pie. I think my hands were sticky and clouded with flour when I remembered to call to schedule your complete x-ray survey and check-up.

Audrey on left, Tracy on right

Chapter 5: Roadblock

Our pediatrician explained that an unmistakable coin lesion was present in your right lung field. It is the pattern of Wilm's to travel from kidney to lung if the disease is metastatic (spreading) in nature. I had no time to ponder a margin of error. Surgery was impending if we all agreed to treat your invasion aggressively. Who could not agree when metastatic Wilm's was hitting you so brutally? Your medical staff put their heads together and decided an injection of vincristine was the first step they would take, since your body had not utilized this potent drug for a month. Hopefully, the drug would hinder the growth, perhaps even shrink it.

About two and a half hours had elapsed since the vincristine had been administered. We "conned" your father into going out to dinner, and maybe a movie. Hence, we stayed in the city. At dinner you said your legs felt weak and you felt sick. I had long been taking even the slightest complaint registered by you most seriously. You were not an undue alarmist. You would have been more likely to say that you were fine at any given time. I became a sentinel evaluating any signal of trouble. Here, is the only point on which I congratulate myself. Somehow, I was given the way to watch you like a private eye without letting my fears show, and thereby making you apprehensive. Soon, you began to vomit profusely. It didn't end even way into the night. (I insisted we stay in a hotel close to the hospital.) During the wee hours, we rushed you to the emergency entrance. It looked like a bad case of stomach flu aggravated by the vincristine. In the reasonable hours of the morning, the vomiting worsened, if anything. A second medical opinion concurred that unfortunately the flu and your medicine were at war with one another.

At home, and in your own bed, the vomiting subsided. Do you recall that eight of our out of state relatives unexpectedly dropped in to visit early that evening? I entered your room quietly, not wanting to disturb your sleep, to find you looking worried and altogether awake. I told you who had come, and inquired if you thought it might make you feel better to visit awhile? "I will, if you carry me out there." . . . Yes, that was your answer. Doubting my ears, (I too, was in need of sleep) I asked if I had heard correctly. You told me that you tried to walk to the bathroom and that your legs just wouldn't go! Mine flew to the telephone to call for Doctor Jim to meet me at Memorial Hospital in the emergency room. Aside from gross dehydration, he sized up the situation to be a whopping adverse reaction to the drug vincristine. You couldn't open your mouth or turn your head. Every inch of your body screamed in pain. Days later, I was introduced to a condition whose name itself commands respect: You suffered from hypo-calcemic tetany. Dr. Couch kept his batting average without blemish. He decided to nearly float you away with fluids loaded with calcium. Some time later, he received a specialist's call from St. Jude's in Memphis suggesting enormous amounts of calcium to restore your body's chemical balance. I chuckled to myself in the face of adversity. The suggestion came after-the-fact. Dear J.C. knew what he was doing with my angel . . . he knew, and He also knew!

Now, all we had to do was to get you well enough for lung surgery. During the bout with "flu," your ego and your self-esteem took an added whipping. Your hair was gone, all but a fringe of bangs. This time you cried and I cried unabashedly. We decided to buy two human hair wigs in a frosted color, because your hair was naturally streaked in that blonde on brown tone. Why the extravagance of two good wigs? Very elementary, when one realizes that you literally had nothing to wear while one hair piece was being cleaned or styled. Your little sister went wig shopping with me to save you further embarrassment. We so often heard comments on your lovely, luxurious hair. I could tell that we managed to fool the public but it was hard to convince you that their compliments were indeed, genuine.

A genteel, southern gentleman and you had a date at Presbyterian in December. The date was not carefree, since he had to remove a wedge from your lung. Pathology studies proved that it was a recurrence of your original illness. Once again you resided in the Intensive Care Unit. I will mention your dread, the abominable chest tube, that seemed to dare you to move or even to breathe, except in a careful shallow manner. And, I will mention your delight, the skillful surgeon who made no pretense about the fact that this Yankee called Tracy Elizabeth was someone very dear to him. The feeling was mutual.

Another drug, dactinomycin, was used for blood therapy. No nectar, this one. It was so intensely cruel to your stomach that retching was commonplace to you. No more a robust, healthy little girl. Your school requirements were met almost entirely through top rate tutoring in our kitchen. My nerves tighten as this period of your life is focused upon. March and June marked your fourth and fifth trips to the operating room, both times for the removal of other isolated lesions in that same poor right lung. Metastatic Wilm's Tumor was the dizzying tune that spun round and round in my weary brain. With each instance, I was reminded that every set back gave you less chance for survival. The underlying thought kept hounding me: Maybe they were right when they said you were too old?

I could not be caught in the web of despair for very long. Your recuperations never ceased to astound everyone. You seemed to defy all the odds by surviving, and more than that by savoring all that life had to offer during the good times. Your attitude never changed. Discharge from any hospital found you ready to hit the books, ride that bike and (now that your hair grew back) jump into the nearest swimming pool.

Chapter 6: Proceed With Caution

Your teacher promoted you to the third grade with an excellent report card for us to treasure. Just before the end of school, you fell at recess and broke your arm. Boy, were you proud. It was such a divinely natural and normal malady. We worried that the cast might never be discarded. It had so many important autographs inscribed, after all!

Our pediatrician was loaded with homey colloquialisms. He was immensely concerned that dactinomycin did such an apparent losing battle. Three surgeries in the past nine months did not exactly look like we might emerge victorious. "We are between a rock and a hard place," was the way he summarized the picture contained in your medical volume.   Usually, I could laugh at the way he expressed himself, but this time was different. He was asking your father and me to agree to use vincristine as your treatment again. A rock and a hard place, indeed, the problem was not easily solved. I was shaking in my seat about this one. Not a single incident involved in the bad reaction to vincristine was erased from my memory. Still we had to agree that trying it again was the best option. A wise decision was made that day.

The initial dosage of the familiar drug was given at two week intervals in a hospital surrounding, rather than on an out patient basis. The calcium and intravenous fluid bottles were never more than a few feet away, should the bad reaction repeat itself. You demonstrated some irritability and some twitching. Always, the calcium lessened these side effects. Hypo-calcemic tetany attacks neuro-muscularly, and you showed a small degree of reaction. (Once, you tried to hit me with your bed pan!) I gritted my teeth, and felt sorry for you instead of for myself. With each dose, those side effects gradually began to disappear. It became safe once again to present you and your veins every second week in the office. A much more settling arrangement.

You asked your Southern gentleman, who was so well acquainted with your lungs, if you would always have to walk "wounded bird style" from the operations that made a huge backward C from mid-chest, under the arm, to mid-back. He said he thought not if you were tough enough to withstand vigorous exercise. I can attest to the fact that my Yankee swung that arm until I thought it surely would fly somewhere into the next county!

There was a method to your madness, dear one, you wanted to continue swimming lessons in order to join your sister and participate, not as a spectator, in a community swim show. That last chest surgery was an impressive one. It had been necessary to remove the whole of the lower lobe of your right lung. Your Mother did suffer some pangs of apprehension, even if you stood firm on the course of remaining fearless. The swimming pool, so soon after your fifth ordeal, represented to me a body of water loaded with sharks and dangerous under-tow! On the other hand, I had a talk with myself, about how the very same pool represented a wonderful source of exercise which provided you with normal, childhood fun. Unknown to you, I spoke privately with the instructors. They would make some excuse believable to you as to why you should not proceed beyond the five feet mark. In addition, they would always omit you (you thought they were extremely absent-minded) in any distance swimming. The evening of the big swim show found this mother applauding her children's efforts so strenuously that the palms of said mother's hands were triumphantly black and blue.

By the end of the summer you girls glowed with attractive suntans. Your fine looking exterior may well have been an omen of what was happening in that all-important interior. It was the start of a miraculous seventeen month remission. Let's hear it for the exciting come-back of periwinkle juice (or vincristine)! Periwinkle blue is my favorite color, white periwinkles blossomed in our front yard, and I vote for periwinkles to be our National Flower. Senators, Congressmen, vote for the periwinkle!

Audrey on left age 6, Tracy on right age 8
photo by J.C.Couch

Chapter 7: Pumpkins and Pilgrims

It was near the end of November and rumors began to circulate that our military base might be closing. When the rumors became factual, we needed to research a compassionate base of choice. We had to live within a reasonable distance of a good medical facility and it appeared that Rome, New York, would be home to us. But first things first: A Thanksgiving Day warrants special prominence. History credits the Pilgrims and the Indians for that first feast of praise in 1621. Ours did not lack in the spirit of giving thanks to the One who provides all our needs. An annual family gathering is set this day in a quaint, old Methodist country church. It was Dr. Jim's family, who ritually kept the custom. How gracious it was for our company of four to be invited to join their celebration. Nearly a hundred people were present, an impressive number for that small sanctuary. Our plates were heaped with turkey, ham, goose, pumpkin pie AND pecan pie, lest anyone forget this observance took place in Oklahoma! At least three ministers presided over us, therefore, it was understandable why so many spontaneous, sincere prayers were offered between helpings.

The nearly impossible part of the day, was not the function of digesting so much food, as would ordinarily be a safe guess. No, it was the real task of saying our goodbyes to Dr. Jim and La Rita Couch and their children. I did surprisingly well until one of their girls looked up at me and said, "But will we EVER see you again?" I couldn't say yes, with any sense of honesty or real conviction, since our car would soon be facing the direction of New York. It's hard to answer a charming young lady untruthfully. I took "plan B," and sobbed a hundred million earnest tears! In attending their family dinner, we set out for New York by driving perhaps two hundred miles in the wrong direction. Now, there's love!

You and Audrey were just as miserable. This page has been written in the same, slow, feet-dragging way that we headed north. We might as well have been driving to our own executions . . . no one spoke . . . occasionally someone whimpered aloud, or blew a feminine nose . . . even Frizzle sensed the somber feeling that had overtaken her family. Out of sheer respect for the mood that prevailed, she did not either wag her tail or bound from lap to lap. It escapes me what finally broke the ice. However, experience tells me that one child had to go to the bathroom. God bless the child!

Chapter 8: White on White on White

We beat the arrival of the first snowfall by only a few days. And, what a blizzard it turned out to be. A ticker-tape parade of welcome, complete with rainbows of confetti, wouldn't have impressed us as did this magnificent frosting of white on white on white! It was great stuff, and we didn't tire of it. If any of nature's gifts compare with the sensation of catching fresh snowflakes with your tongue . . . or with that exhilarating feeling when free-falling back into several feet of snow (first step in creating angels fluttering their wings) . . . I guess we never discovered those gifts!

There was another bonus connected with residing in Rome, New York. For the first time, visiting Grandma and Grandpa and dear Aunt Kay was not a monumental task, preceded by hours of packing and days of travel to our destination. It was a beautiful lesson in geography to discover that we were not-too-distant neighbors to Pennsylvania. Holidays took on a whole new meaning, didn't they? Now we could enjoy them with beloved relatives.

For the first time we decided not to live on the military reservation. We elected to buy a house situated in a country setting. You especially loved your very own hills and wooded areas that became your playground. And, it wounded none of us (when the seasons changed) to have a good friendship with the people next door, who just happened to possess that inviting swimming pool! You and Audrey boarded the school bus each morning already taking for granted your good health. That year there were no interruptions due to hospitalizations. Third grade was a breeze.

BIZARRE . . . that is the word one of your new doctors used to describe you. Your medication had to continue on a regular basis, so we presented ourselves to the highly respected Syracuse University Hospital for your care. The first time there, slim little Audrey was lifted to the examining table. "Wrong girl, doctor," came tumbling out of my mouth . . . "BIZARRE," was his profound reply. He found it difficult to comprehend certain little truths about you: that you attended school regularly; that you went sledding regularly; that you roller-skated and jumped rope regularly. On one occasion, the same expert reminded me that only "SICK" children were seen on Tuesdays. A history of metastatic Wilm's was sufficient to keep you a "Tuesday's Child." But, I have always felt proud that to the expert you appeared bizarre, rather than sick. Medical science needs an occasional jolt like you . . . an eccentric, flamboyant, altogether gorgeous rebel who refuses to fit into the likely mold that unfortunately "fits" too many of the chronically ill in this world. I am convinced that you secretly had more than one belly-laugh, as I did, when history repeated itself. Similar reactions occurred, and other specialists could seldom contain their utter amazement when confronted with this delightful, but puzzling, girl. We can both think back, with amusement, about the expressions worn by the people who worked in the Department of Nuclear Medicine. They must have been pleased with your progress, and, at the same time, perplexed with your progress!

Meanwhile, back on the home front, important discoveries were being uncovered. It was a world of whirring snowmobiles outdoors. Yes, snowmobiles and skis and hot chocolate and trees being tapped for maple syrup. It seemed a good time to expose my girls to some culture, as well. So, you both began piano lessons. You came along very nicely in this endeavor, but a serious student you were not. I took several pictures of the pose that you assumed in front of the piano for practice, in an effort to encourage a better posture. Alas! That failed to bring rewards. You continued to sit on your right foot, with the left foot dangling nowhere near the pedals. Maybe you intended to play comic duets with Victor Borge some day, who knows?

In reading thus far, the impression may be misleading. New York does not have floor to ceiling snow the year round. In fact, every season is thrilling with a different kind of beauty to surround its inhabitants. I made the observation that there is a postcard scene available to the discerning eye in every direction. The Autumn season was the grand masterpiece. I had appreciated fall foliage before in shades of gold, brown and red. But, the Adirondack Mountains show leaves in vibrant yellow tones, not to mention burgundy and even hot pink! Our artistic senses couldn't lie dormant for any period of time, neither could interest in things historical be lagging. No, not with the Erie Canal, and reminders of the Revolutionary War prodding you to open the encyclopedia again and again. It turned out to be great that your daddy's job allowed you to see still another part of your country. It was a "patriotic" time in your life. Why, even Francis Bellamy Grade School was named for the man who gave us the Pledge of Allegiance. (Some reference books do not give him sole credit.) However, it was something to whet your scholastic appetite.

We moved again, back to a familiar setting. Once again we were residents of on-base housing. The house that we originally selected in upstate New York was a bit out of reach financially. I was fearful that you would miss the wide open spaces, and the rural charm. This was not the case at all. You had become so accustomed to multiple-family dwellings, that you exhaled a happy sigh of security. Both you and Audrey agreed that it was swell to have street lights at night. And, in unison, a cheer resounded for SIDEWALKS! I never thought much about a fascination for cement. But, if riding bikes and roller-skating were tops on the list of priorities, then it makes sense to long for smooth sidewalks.

Being back on base was neat for you in another respect. Wherever you were, you knew it was time to come home when the National Anthem resounded at dusk. Children in the housing area were taught to stand still and to put their hands over their hearts for the duration of the song. It was stirring and comforting for you to feel that 'the flag was still there.' I proudly watched and witnessed your sincerity as you sang, "O say, does that star-spangled banner yet wave o'er the land of the free (drum roll) and the home of the brave?" Of course, everyone stopped mid stride wherever they were, no matter what they were doing, but it was the children that gave me goose bumps. One of your best friends, the Chaplain's son, took his patriotism a step further. He was in the bathtub when he scarcely heard the anthem's strains. His mom found him standing hand over heart in his "nuders." I always thought that little anecdote needed to find its way into *Reader's Digest*!

It takes very little effort to delight basically happy children. Halloween is a very good case in point. We spent just as much time in the selection of pumpkins for jack-o-lanterns, as we allotted to the choice of the right tree to decorate for Christmas. If the face is to be funny or cute . . . a round pumpkin is required. On the other hand, if a scary, ghoulish face is to be achieved . . . the oblong shape is a must. You were adept at carving praise-worthy jack-o-lanterns by yourself for, perhaps, two years. After trick or treating around the neighborhood, I usually filled the kitchen sink to brimming, to let you girls bob for apples until your ears were water-logged. Then, a nice cup of hot apple cider with several doughnuts was the traditional bed-time snack to ward off evil witches or dreams of skeletons.

A future Halloween would prove to be gloomy and very depressing. I would have only one girl thinking about the holiday. When Audrey and I ate the usual snack, your absence was more like a painful unmistakable presence. Anyway, dear heart, we missed that infectious, soprano-giggle. On Sunday afternoon the sadness was dispelled. After church, I inquired of your sister how she would feel about putting the "cute" pumpkin on your grave. Her first reaction was, "what??" Then, in a very few moments, she decided that was the perfect thing to do. She thought it would bring a smile to your heavenly face. That is why your grave was adorned with a child's hewn jack-o-lantern, and some beautifully colored Indian corn. Maybe our idea wasn't customary or readily grasped by conformists, but it did serve to bring us over the first holiday without you. And, if Mommy knows you, then you were indeed wearing a special grin on that All Saints' Day.

Chapter 9: Bedlam

Isn't it strange the way so many memories, good or bad, seem to fall on designated holidays? You began to show pain in the peculiar way that you walked. Emptying your bladder hurt too. As I stated previously, you tended to under-play any discomfort. I bombarded you with questions, and my eyes were glued to your every movement, every change in expression. The morning of Thanksgiving you and I took a tense ambulance ride to the big medical center. You had a tremendous mass in that well explored abdomen. I shook, Honey, but I was not taken completely by surprise. There was another problem that did make me reel, though. Another lesion was found, this one in your "good" left lung. Now you were no longer bizarre . . . to the contrary, you were, indeed sick! They were giving up on my daughter. At this encounter with tragic symptoms, the voices spoke compassionately. It appeared we had reached a state with you where supportive, palliative measures could only be offered. "What happened to aggressive treatment?" I demanded to know. With your recuperative powers, I wanted them to talk about curing you. Keeping you comfortable was absurd! I then had a talk with Doctor Couch. He had already conferred with our pediatrician. Four or five minds came to the same conclusion finally, and the ambulance transferred you to a larger city, Buffalo, for evaluation at Roswell Park Hospital. I knew that this was your chance to grab on to a miracle. Only now could I unwind enough to cry and to pray.

You used to say that this place made your stomach turn over. I shared your sentiments. I remember so vividly that we did journey via an ambulance to the hospital. You were far too uncomfortable to ride a spirited stallion that day! The first thing for me to do was to admit you . . . Okay, I had done that on many occasions in many hospitals. The catch: It was necessary on each admission to agree to a post-mortem examination on the patient. Perhaps I'm an old softie, but I found that a tough one to overcome. I loved you, and I wanted to feel that a post-mortem wouldn't become a necessity. We had brought a suitcase full of nighties and robes and slippers, because it seemed the proper apparel for an ill person. The catch: Patients were expected to wear skirts and slacks and shoes . . . Did we want you to think of yourself as being "sick?" There is that word again! Not wishing to disturb the natural order of things, I rushed to a busy department store, and hurriedly selected a heavy armful of play clothes in shades complimentary to you. The catch: A sales girl exerting all the authority of George C. Scott inferred that she had every reason to assume that I had shoplifted several items . . . After all I was in a suspicious frantic sort of haste, wasn't I? Forgive me, darling, for injecting angry sarcasm into your story here . . . but, you and I seemed to be the only ones genuinely concerned with your welfare at a time when a terribly alarming picture of your prognosis was hitting us head-on. Your Mommy has always been blessed with a side-ways kind of funny bone. It is called Gallows Humor. The catch: Sometimes I am misunderstood to be a hard Momma. Sometimes, too, people think me unbalanced. Now, I know that you are laughing, because the love that we shared with one another knew no flaws. So much for beautiful, downtown Buffalo. Thank you, all of you!

At first, your new battery of physicians decided to use a different drug, combined with radiation therapy where it was needed. This decision surely couldn't harm . . . but would it achieve that essential cure? Several days later, a confident (nearly cocky) young surgeon came from another hospital to investigate this puzzling youth with her man-sized problems. He studied you... he studied me... and then he said, "If she were my daughter I would operate to attempt the total removal of that mass in her belly, which you say is enlarging by the day. Next, if she were mine I would want that lung irradiated." I suppose he expected a delay in my reply. This person knew within himself that he had come on strong. My answer tumbled off my tongue to the affirmative after having swallowed just once! I told the surgeon later, that his magic words had been: "If she were my daughter . . . if she were mine" . . . I had not heard anything so personal or so appealing since we left Oklahoma. And, it did nothing but enhance his charisma, when a midwestern accent was so easily detected.

Honey, you were in Buffalo, in yet another hospital, awaiting your sixth trip to the operating room, and you were scared. Daddy and I were stiff with worry and fright. But, you never knew this, because I very calmly read passages from the Bible to you. Psalm 121 seemed to fit all our immediate needs. I can cite some of the chapter: "My help comes from the Lord who made heaven and Earth . . . He who watches over you and Israel will neither slumber nor sleep . . . The sun will not harm you by day, nor the moon by night. The Lord will keep you from all harm; He will watch over your life. The Lord will keep your going out and your coming in both now and for evermore." I kissed you, tucked the Bible under your small arm, told you I loved you, rode the elevator downstairs with you and pointed to where I would either sit or stand all the while you were in surgery. When those heavy doors closed, I sank. The façade of calmness and super-human confidence always speedily left just as soon as you were completely out of my hands. Although I never strayed more than a room away as the specialists labored, it nearly killed me to give you to them. I would much rather have watched the entire drama in the operating rooms on all six occasions, than to have experienced the feelings of disconnected helplessness.

The mid-westerner beamed when his job was done. He told us that the mass was self-contained, even though it was a huge twelve centimeters or more. He likened it to a soccer ball. Positively a successful goal had been reached. He went on and on about how he effortlessly was able to lift out, almost pluck off, the Wilm's metastasis. Some precautionary radiation would be aimed at your tummy, then we'd have to see about that lung in time for Christmas. Another lightening fast recovery took place. You'd done it before, let's have another encore, champ!

Back at Roswell Park, a new agent was begun in chemotherapy. It was red, the name begins with the letter, A. We shall refer to it as "your red poison." It was so toxic, I can't think of a better nickname. You had become thin on this poison. You "vomited your socks up," in your own words. Your crowning glory thinned quite noticeably, however, we were armed with two natural looking wigs should the worst happen. The red poison combined with the x-ray treatments to your chest proved effective. The process was so extremely slow, it must be noted that significant change in your lung lesion wasn't apparent until three believers in Christ prayed specifically for your healing. Then, like a flash, your lung-field was clear. The credit goes, of course, to "A" or adriamycin, and to the wonders of radiation therapy, and to your new staff of intelligent doctors. But, if I had failed to give praise to God for His mercy and for His ears that responded to prayer, I would have been the prime example of the village idiot!

Chapter 10: On Wheels

Deck them halls, Grandma, we are coming to Valley View for Christmas. You were still wearing your hospital identification bracelet on December 23rd, but not on Christmas Eve, my dear! We rode by bus the many miles to our small community in Pennsylvania. (We, being the girls of the family.) Daddy drove by himself . . . ah, but he was not entirely alone. The car was low to the ground, as it bore the weight of a sleigh full of packages which were destined to find their place under the pretty tree.

So many fools in the world! The long bus ride showed us an appreciable number of them. To many poor creatures, Christmas is just another cue to break the seal of a bottle of cheer. The bottles I saw being passed from degenerate to degenerate contained not a smidgeon of cheer. I was sorry I had inadvertently exposed my children to the madness that went on before our eyes. Men made suggestive advances to females of any age ... boys ran to the bathroom to heave loudly from their over-indulgence . . . at least three fist fights had to be stopped by the driver . . . and, this Mother came surprisingly close to hitting a young man who shouted profane and gutter words at me every time I opened the window just a crack to let us breathe some fresh, odor-free air.

All was calm about ten o'clock that night, when the bus was dark. I invited some children to join me in singing Christmas carols. After several renditions of "Rudolph" and "Frosty," and

"Santa Claus is Coming to Town," the prevailing atmosphere was joyous. In the cloak of darkness, adults became as children . . . No one could see who fell under the magic that IS Christmas . . . burdensome inhibitions were cast aside. I soloed with "Oh, Holy Night" from the back of the bus. What did I care about critics, when this was the only time my children and I had been together since before Thanksgiving? No one applauded, but no one cursed me, either. A voice belonging to some person near the front of the vehicle asked if we knew "O Little Town of Bethlehem?" We sang it . . . Then we sang "Silent Night" . . . Then another favorite, and on and on it went. One old man who had been very, very drunk earlier told me that he had not paid any attention to, or sung those carols since he was in the second grade. It was he who led us all in a boisterous, "Joy To The World!" I am crying and laughing at the same time right this minute, just as I did then. Oh, Sweetheart, I know that night held precious meaning to you; do not forget it!

The birthday cake says Tracy is ten. You didn't feel well on your day, after the course of red poison. We went to a nice restaurant and ordered lobster tail, your favorite, which I ate, because when it was put before you, you felt nauseated. It had been our practice for the birthday person to have whatever he or she desired for dinner that day. You had matured from peanut butter sandwiches, to hot dogs, to steak, to lobster. In a very few days after your birthday, your hair was gone for the second time. This time you really rebelled. After all, a lovely pre-teen Miss does have some pride and vanity. When the shock had subsided, we found that it was possible to cajole you in the form of gentle flattery. I showed you baby pictures from way back, and told you that it made me feel like a young Mommy again to look at you sans hair . . . you hadn't changed a bit, you retained that adorable baby-face. I reminded you quite sincerely that hair sometimes hid real character and good looks. I made a special point of wearing my wig a lot. We dubbed ourselves the twins when our "rugs" rested at night on our respective bedposts. Who can be plagued with hair styles in a Volkswagen that shuffled off to Buffalo every twelve days for treatment? You even allowed me to massage, very vigorously, that head of yours. And, we chuckled together every time I said it was time to "wake up the flavor!" Audrey was a doll, in that she frequently wore your alternate wig. Both of you were fashion setters.

It is still white and crispy winter. For the countless trips to the hospital, weather decided our mode of travel. The old reliable train coughed us there when more than three feet of snow blanketed the ground. Didn't we enjoy those train excursions? We took sandwiches and California oranges for supper, since the train's scheduled departure was five o'clock p.m. (Laugh inserted here!) Ten o'clock was the earliest arrival time in Buffalo EVER . . . on this scheduled three hour run. Even today when I search for a decent pair of pantyhose, my train experiences are foremost in my mind. Nearly every pair has "suitcase knees" . . . a phrase I used to describe how "dimples" appeared in all of my hosiery. Do you suppose that commuters also wear suitcase knees in their business slacks? I don't know, but someday I intend to check this out.

The red poison was working well enough for you to resume school now on the fourth grade level. You and Audrey began ballet lessons about this time from the dearest instructor in the world. He led you, like the magical Piper, into the five basic positions. You girls lived ballet, took the whole process so extremely seriously. The living room had to be shoved about often as you needed plenty of room to exercise those graceful glissades, passés and the dizzying chaîné turns. At first, you hesitated in joining Audrey to learn the basics of ballet. I learned that your fear was that your hair might fall off during the leaps, or worse, at the finish of a grand reverence bow! We remedied the possibility by having you wear colorful tight headbands. It was never my habit to inform people of your illness, but the truth was made known to your lovable Irish dance instructor one day when he casually mentioned how both of you really excelled in your endeavors. He lauded Audrey's gracefulness, and your impeccable posture. That was all he said, so it understandably confused him when my taut throat left me speechless, and I turned from him to hide the tears that would not cease to flow. When you both danced out of ear range, I explained to him that it moved me so to know that he considered your posture worth mention and praise. You certainly avoided the inevitable "wounded bird" stance. Your shoulders were straight. Another victory for you! Too, I told him of your dread that the wig would be detected, because he raved about your beautiful hair. Well, dear, we had an ally ready to defend you against that one clumsy "stomper" who questioned you incessantly about your hair. I told you she was green with envy at an early age . . . probably because she was powerless over her "horse face."

The train was fun for both of us. We played countless bouts of hang-man, got caught up with homework, and sang all the songs we ever knew. If and when boredom set in, we'd stagger from car to car in the best carriage we could master. We'd try to copy the walks of the conductors, but that was when we'd lose our balance altogether. Our sustenance differed . . . a kind of generation gap . . . you'd have solid gold peanuts for your expensive treat, I'd sometimes have a beer. Let's hope that one pause for liquid refreshment won't wound my esteem in the Bible Belt!

There was nothing wrong with our morale going to the hospital. Once inside their doors, though, I felt the black cloud of doom. My first chore was always to agree to your post-mortem exam. If my pulse raced so breathlessly, why oh why did my blood just run cold and stop each and every time I had to sign my hideous name. I grew to despise my name more with each admission to the hospital. There were a goodly number of admissions, because the type A poison usually caused you to vomit to the point of dehydration. In the hospital we made many cherished young friends with problems similar to yours. The wee ones referred to me as, "Tracy's Mommy," a title I liked immensely. I might add I do not ever intend to tarnish its significance.

On two occasions I found you upset when visiting hours were in effect. It was unlike you to allow negative pressures to surface. You took me aside and whispered to me shakily that little Lisa had leukemia, or Hodgkin's, or Mikey's limb would be amputated because he had bone cancer. You never revealed to me the source of information, but you felt so blue about these illnesses. My head would scream silently that if you only knew of your own serious disease . . . Then, I'd snap back to reality relieved of the decision made years before, that above all, you would not know how unsure was the possibility of a future in store for you. You had seen boxes upon boxes of white mice, and quizzed me about them. I could see no reason to avoid answering that a large part of this hospital was devoted to research to ultimately wipe out cancers of all kinds. This astounded you and you couldn't wait to tell your teacher and the class that YOUR hospital might succeed in defeating this buzzard of a disease. Now, Roswell Park ranked in importance with Jerry Lewis and his campaign against muscular dystrophy.

Looking back when our lives were much simpler, I remember the Labor Day Telethon going on as we were preparing to relocate to Oklahoma. We were waist high in boxes that needed to be packed deciding this goes, this stays, when your interest in what Jerry was doing for "his kids" became so piqued that we dropped everything and joined the mass of door to door solicitors. You and Audrey worked so diligently that at the end of the day you both were interviewed by the local television studio. You were singled out because you were such little girls who did the formidable job of collecting the most money for M.D.A. I recall your victories with satisfaction every Labor Day. I plan to walk in your stead as long as I can. This is a deed that will change a day of grief to a day of purpose. It is well to remind anew that a little child may lead the way.

At the tender age of seven, the drugs, along with the tedious hospitalizations, became a heavy load for one so small to carry. As this repeated itself sometimes you became despondent for a few minutes. You summed the whole mess up with a brief cure-all, "I should never have been born." That statement stung me hard, but it had been revised some. At just six, your grammar, not always perfect, your summation was, "You should never have borned me, Mommy." That message didn't sting, it cut, and I bled with despair that you should ever have felt this way! Your dark moods only prevailed for short minutes from time to time.

Twice you attempted self-diagnosis. Just following the third chest surgery I came breezing in to call on my favorite patient, wearing my super-happy face. Both feet had not yet entered your room when you blurted out "Do I have lung cancer" . . . This was said as a statement, there wasn't any question in your voice. I had an urgent need to go to the bathroom (to muster up my composure, and unruffle my feathers) after which I asked you what prompted such a strange greeting. It was the idiot box with the most important news item of the week. Some celebrity had died shortly after thoracic surgery. I then asked if the news media reported that the patient had smoked to excess, and that he also suffered from advanced emphysema? You countered with an up and down nod of the head. "Okay, young lady, let's discuss how many cigarettes you've been sneaking." You laughed very, very hard and apologized for daring to entertain such silly notions.

Your own diagnoses came up more than once as your years increased. You really did suspect that your serious illness was leukemia, because of the way that your blood was always of utmost interest to the medical establishment. To heighten your suspicions, you came across an article about a child who was leukemic. She was pictured receiving intravenous vincristine. The article went on to explain how vincristine was derived in part from the genus vinca, or periwinkle. Wow! My only means of persuasion was to call your attention to the many "zippers" (incision scars) you had acquired, and to tell you that patients with leukemia were not fortunate enough to have operations save them. Your worries left you!

The tracks were heading homeward, our camera-eyes panned the view that a train window swiftly affords its passengers. Your radio had annoying static that afternoon, so we agreed to sing some of our favorite tunes. After at least half a dozen renditions had been sung: selections like "Raindrops Keep Fallin' On My

Head" and "I'll Never Fall In Love Again," I noticed an attractive lady smiling in our direction. She was seated just across the aisle from us. We thought we had only been entertaining each other. But this woman had most receptive ears. She had heard every tune above the muffled clatter of the train ride. We both knew by her expression that she had not been annoyed, but why she so obviously enjoyed our concert remained a question for several more minutes. We arrived at the conclusion that she must be a talent scout, and we had been auditioned and discovered at last! Well, not quite. The public would have to be deprived of a lyric and mezzo soprano duo for a little while. As it happened, our entire musical repertoire was solid Burt Bacharach, and this nice lady turned out to be his secretary. She was en route back to the desk in New York City. Ah, so near and yet so far!

It is now very early in March. As the season changed, our mode of travel changed going to and from the hospital. Our green VW bug was perfect for Spring. Honey, can you look back on our lengthy trips (only the two of us) and see how squeezably close we became? Really, our complete love and understanding was never better. We'd jump into the bug and say in unison, "If God be for us, who can be against us." So many times I'd yawn and stretch and become "too fatigued" to drive any further without your able assistance. You would steer that automobile at normal speeds on the thru-way, or wield it into a parking spot along the way when we needed fuel for it, or for us. This was a tremendous help to me, because I could doze off when merely my foot was required. The secret had better be uncovered lest the law comes bearing tickets and shouting violation! Only my right eye dozed (the one that was visible to you) Hence, with my head tipped back in that restful pose, I could see quite well. You took your responsibility seriously, and you executed the steering admirably. For the record, I would not recommend this procedure for the average ten year old, but it has long been established that you were never average. You were born extraordinary. I rest my case!

A funny thing happened on the New York Thru-way. It seems apparent enough that countless unfunny incidents occur making the news. With this in mind let me enlighten you. We came to a slow but sure stop. This halt was not in our plans, but there we were, moving zero miles per hour. It is the rule that when in distress, one locks all doors, turns on flashing lights and dangles something white from the closed window. Neither of us had anything on our persons decent enough to dangle from the window in living-white. (Are we laughing?) You and I thought the whole situation a roaring joke. We sat there doing nothing constructive. So, it was no surprise that assistance didn't hurry by. Time passed, and we kept all our clothes on. Not too many light years later, a gallant modern day knight intentionally brought his horse power to a whoa. Next, said knight tapped on our window mouthing something that we interpreted as "May I help you?" The rule book said never trust a stranger, therefore we set our eyes straight ahead ignoring the outsider. Undaunted, he tapped out the same message, this time with an exaggerated grin on his face. He was, of course, trying to appeal to my little girl and to me as harmless as saccharine. Ignore the dirty old man and he'll go away. A man is innocent until proven guilty, right? He wasn't dirty or old or the least bit sinister looking. These were but a few reasons that we decided to ALLOW the good man to find the problem with our car. We ran out of gas! What else can I tell you? Our pal decided to siphon gasoline from his tank. His equipment was something to write about. We worked together like a trained team. He held a pouch attached to some clear tubing at the proper level. My job was to clamp off the tube when he gave the order . . . He said I handled this with professional aplomb. It was a slow process, with numerous trips from car to car, but eventually we were refueled. Honestly, my pal produced castile soap and a soft towelette for us to clean up. I HAD to ask him if he was always prepared for any emergency that might arise. The gallant one grinned again, as he revealed that he was a hospital supply salesman, and we had just utilized the very latest in disposable enema tools. He bade us farewell, as he rode off into the sunset. It was getting late, very late. We talked about our good fortune and the kind salesman, then we laughed like loons at the saga of the New York Thru-way.

It is March eighth, Frizzle is five . . . more importantly, Audrey is eight years old. There were presents, to be sure, but the issue that counted was dinner for the birthday girl. Audrey wanted to go to Grandma and Grandpa's house to dine at a small restaurant near there. Authentic Pennsylvania Dutch meals were featured. Audrey's order was a hot turkey sandwich, thank you very much. Daddy didn't join us in the fun. He chose not to share in any family activity for weeks previous to this birthday. I have not forgotten who this story is about. Just let me briefly mention a solemn death within the family. It was the total demise of our marriage. Way back, Mommy and Daddy said with real conviction, "'til death do us part." Following years of non-communication, we had progressed to communicating with hostility and pain. A legal separation was initiated, with divorce to become final in the summer. Your reactions were slightly different, as I'm quite sure you can recall. You stated your position on the subject like an unbiased newsperson. You truthfully and calmly told me that you had been expecting it, and you thought it best for all of us. Audrey spent a short time weeping enormous tears before she reached the same conclusion. She wisely predicted less terrible headaches for Mommy. Several days later, she wanted to tell me why she cried. Her concerns had a religious basis. She needed to know if she could still honor her father, and would Daddy still BE her father? I answered affirmatively to both questions. We so often referred to Audrey as the little missionary, because her world was simple and good, and quite resolute. Now we may return to your story. Not one wicked witch turned Dad into a frog. Okay? Okay!

Chapter 11: Your Essence

You would march into Roswell for treatment clad in the most hip apparel. Your personality blended completely with boots and hot pants, ponchos and shoulder bags. You also leaned toward a prairie dress, with open sandals under a long multi-colored skirt. All who glimpsed you in your very favorite outfits knew that this girl had style! It takes an exuberant flair to wear a brilliant red gaucho set, complete with a navy suede cummerbund. *Women's Wear Daily* should have been allowed the spectacular vision of a model with no experience, yet who could effortlessly BE the girl inside whatever clothes she "felt like" on a given day.

Part of your accessories included a small wooden peace symbol attached to a chain necklace. You wore this every day since it had been given to you at a hospital Christmas party. The Santa who won your heart came from the North Pole by way of Latin America. When he said the expected, "Ho, ho, ho, this is Santa Claus," it sounded undeniably sexy. One must only stretch the imagination to hear these familiar words as if they were spoken by Antonio Banderas. In reality, the Argentinean man (who shook when he laughed) was one of the doctors unable to conceal his endearing love for children.

We are late into March, and you spent a few days alone with your grandparents for the first and only time. Your sister had savored this treat on a few occasions when your appointments had to be kept with the medical people. Grandma told me that you had been such a delight. Also, that it was a revelation that would remain for her, to discover first-hand the two faces of my darling. One was wise and understanding beyond your chronological age. The other was a teasing elf who was provoked to giggling at almost anything. You had followed grandma into the master bedroom to watch her "put on her face." Grandma mentioned the moles that peppered her face, and said that she really ought to have at least some of them removed. Then she added that the thought of the procedure scared her. This conversation was intended to be light and casual. She was, in a manner of speaking, addressing herself. But, you had paid attention, and had given the matter substantial consideration. "Are you really afraid, Grandma?" She nodded... and went on powdering . "Then do what my mommy does, read your bible and pray about it, and you'll see that you won't be the least bit scared." You revealed to my mother that day how much this ritual had calmed us in the face of near terror. All the life lessons that I taught you were learned well. You made me proud.

Chapter 12: Bittersweet

April was midway spent when I received a call from the chief of your department at the hospital. His news was of the bad variety, in that a new lesion was quite evident in the right lung field. He feared that the trouble descended into the diaphragm, and perilously close to the liver. Radiation therapy had to begin the very next day, and a new drug would be considered. I knew full well that we were headed for much distress, partly because of the note of deep concern in the doctor's voice... and because, for the first time, I had noticed a genuine warning signal even before his call. You had difficulty breathing on exertion. This illness that we were dealing with was sneaky and cunning. It is most proficient at invading a body, sometimes conquering a body, without the decency of leaving a "calling card" or a kind of symptom to report to your physician. I find myself wanting to curse in order to adequately describe the disease, but no! You never lowered yourself to its reptile-level, and neither will I.

Now we resided in Buffalo more than in our own home. Since your care was again given on an outpatient basis, if we wanted to sleep, we had to buy our beds! The city looms as one giant hospital... In actuality, I was quite aware of five giant medical facilities in the immediate area. The people were ill, very ill...most of the patients required someone to look after them. Does all of this clarify that we were not partying... we were not jet setting...

we were not even tourists vacationing. Part of my blood was donated often at the blood bank, the remainder of my "blood" was spilled in paying outrageous rates in motels, inns, guest houses and such, whose managers began to look like cold, inanimate adding machines. We had been turned away from guest houses after telling the "matrons" that we would need accommodations for five nights. Why should they accept our "pint of blood" when they could be guaranteed gallons, in the cases of some poor souls who lingered long in their terminal situations? The waitresses, with rare exceptions, behaved as medieval boors. They banged our plates and flatware in front of us, and seemed annoyed when we chanced an occasional "please" or "thank you." Rather than offend the offensive ones, we munched together, chatted together and left no tips. That was how we dealt with boors!

You received two big gifts before the calendar was flipped to May. Your teacher promoted you in advance to the fifth grade. This promotion was honestly earned, not merely handed over to you. Mother Frizzle showed us how puppies are born. She presented the family with her second litter of wire fox terriers. They were hysterical and handsome at the same time. You and Audrey nearly required a derrick to lift you out of the basement, and away from those cuddly canines. Frizzle remembered from the first litter how tenderly you handled her babies. So, this time she outdid herself, allowing each of you two puppies to hold.

May sixteenth was exciting indeed. It was the day my girls made their ballet debut at their dance recital. It's anyone's guess which two ballerinas stole the show? With parental bragging out of the way, I really do want to commend you on a job beautifully and expertly done. Your dad surprised us by being there that afternoon. Though we were seated apart, I could feel and see his pride. He applauded your efforts with sincere vigor.

Grandma's family reunion was scheduled for May 31st. You presented yourself for radiation treatment, then off we flew to Pennsylvania. We had been airborne for a short while, when the loudest BOOM made every passenger think of a bomb. We then lost compression, the air ducts became automatic ice makers pelting everyone in their necks... the flight attendant secured herself in her seat for eternity, just as the pilot announced that we would be making an emergency landing. You and Audrey had chosen to sit together, with me across the aisle. The only "cool" lost between you, was when Audrey needed to use the ladies' room, and I instructed her to do the next best thing! Wild conversation went on inside that plane. I asked the trembling man next to me if he had any luggage... he said that he had just bought several new suits in Buffalo... "Well, they are now going over Niagara Falls," was my insipid reply. He then hazarded a question in my direction, something about how I could remain so calm. I told him that I had boarded the plane, leaving behind the leper colony that we so often frequented. I held fast to the image of serenity as he thought about what was just said, and shook violently...there was one woman, whose name I'll never know, who inspired me mid air that day. Through it all she never missed a word in the book she was reading, *Rosemary's Baby!* I suppose it would be anti-climactic to add that we had seen *Airport* one week prior to this flight. The emergency landing was handled with every discretion. Passengers were told that somehow the door to the baggage compartment had blown open in flight. My nervous seatmate was totally impressed with your mommy... how did she ever fathom that this man's luggage might possibly have been swept over the Falls?

A successful and fun-filled day was in progress at the family reunion. You girls enjoyed such a big time, especially during those competitive games that called for team esprit de corps, usually girls versus boys. The flock gathers in a small park that seems to grow greener and more charming with each year. Valley View Park is nestled so close to the mountain range, that it is a chore to visually separate the trees from the forest. At home, you whizzed merrily by onlookers, as you drove Grandpa's ride 'em mower with no help at all. The single photograph I look at from time to time, shows a riding mower with a slightly blurred, radiant Tracy in command of the situation. There is no blur over your facial expression. That big smile is visually intact.

Meanwhile, back at the hospital, a new drug was started. This one is known by a series of letters, BCNU. We called it <u>B</u>reakfast <u>C</u>ocktail <u>N</u>ot <u>U</u>sual. It didn't seem as unkind to you as the type A poison. Yes, you stayed pretty much nauseated and suffered stomach cramps. But, on the other side of the coin, we shared a great secret… you were growing your own hair again. Under that wig, your major prayer was being answered. You asked for your own hair by the summer, to allow you the freedom of swimming without a bathing cap.

My hopes were high, and so were yours. The combination of chemotherapy and radiation had never failed in your case. In addition to that, you felt just plain good, except when <u>B</u>reakfast <u>C</u>ocktail <u>N</u>ot <u>U</u>sual slowed you down for a few uncomfortable days. We had plans to make regarding our next home. I think it not too unrealistic to state that you and Audrey must only have deliberated thirty minutes before deciding that for us it was destination: Oklahoma. I felt that the return to Doctor Couch, and to other friends that we dearly missed, would somehow compensate for leaving your daddy behind. In fact, he left all of us behind when he changed his residence to a room in a boarding house. Doctor Jim had stayed current on your amazing case, so there would be no urgent need for tests and evaluations to determine your future care. I agreed to allow you and your sister to give news releases as to where we would be living to a certain, select group of your best buddies.

I can't describe to you the emotion within me, late in June, when I was called in for a consultation with two of your doctors. It was then that I learned that this mass was hard and resistant. The Wilm's cells had persisted against all medical efforts, and had indeed gotten a strangle-hold on a large portion of your liver. This was the first time that I had really seen your situation as terminal, hopeless. My fortitude and punch left me that afternoon… but, I would see to it that you would keep your perseverance intact. I was advised that you couldn't expect to live. Also, that we needed to leave for Oklahoma soon (by jet) if your wish to live in Oklahoma was to be granted. Honey, I believed these doctors just as surely as I had believed Doctor Couch when he first met you. The heartache and the total resignation were the same. I remembered those feelings only too well. At this point in your life, the positive reasons to "tell the patient" were revealed to me in an altogether well intended gesture. I declined emphatically! You would be told that you were more seriously ill than ever before, and that it would be a tremendous puzzle to find the correct treatment for you. Nothing more was said. Someone in New York had finally listened to me, had actually honored a frantic request. This, in itself, was a relief. I could breathe a little easier now, and face you as I always had. We resumed a normal, loving mother-daughter relationship... a precious intertwining that I did not want to be severed at this late date.

As previously mentioned, you felt great. The sun decided to shine for you, enabling you to swim (without a cap) to your heart's content! I marveled at the way you gave yourself a real workout daily in the pool. You showed absolutely no fatigue. The swimming increased your appetite in a very healthy, natural way. Your ballet instructor took us out for pizza July fifth. We inhaled it like starving refugees. Remember? We anxiously anticipated July eighth to make the scene. That was the day we would fly off in a jet plane for Oklahoma ("where the skies are not cloudy all day").

The next few days proved hectic, but endurable. Future plans clicked in our minds steadily, as we watched our household possessions swiftly being sealed into cartons, then loaded into the enormous moving van. We needed a place to rest our weary bodies for several days and nights before our departure. Mommy rested by the hotel pool; you and Audrey stayed wrinkled and wet. I was able to see both girls from the neck up, as occasionally you would bob up and down long enough to smilingly say "hello!"

*Tracy, 8 years, riding Grandpa's
antique mower in Pennsylvania*

Chapter 13: Heartbreak

It was so abruptly that pain gripped you... We were all taken by surprise. I called your favorite physician from Roswell Park, and reported that your face revealed intolerable pain, and that you walked very guardedly. You had been able to empty your bladder only when nearly submerged in a hot tub of water. He drew a question mark verbally that afternoon. He did not dare to presume that another "problem" had so hastily grown in still another area of your dear human frame! He suggested that I have you checked for a possible cystitis (urinary infection) and obtain something strong enough to relieve your discomfort for tomorrow's journey. You were given demerol, and on rectal examination, it was decided that a pelvic tumor was besieging you.

Grandma and Grandpa came to drive us to the airport, but when they witnessed your condition, tried to persuade us all to stay east. We talked about it, but you and I were in complete accord. You would tough it out, as you had so often done, and we would entrust your care to Doctor Jim. I will never be sorry for the decision we made. If you had desired to fly to Persia, your mommy gladly would have chartered the carpet.

The trip was four grueling hours off schedule. As the length of time increased, your distress increased. It became necessary to call ahead at each stop for a wheel chair. I doubled the dosage of your medicine after calling Doctor Couch, and at 1:30 a.m., we found La Rita and her daughters waiting patiently to drive us home. It was not, in the remotest sense, a joy ride . . . but, thank God, we had arrived!

The Couch abode was known to be a port in anyone's storm. Sometimes it was just their practice of leaving doors unlocked when they were out of town, that calmed one. Neighbors were welcome to help themselves to anything they needed and then return those items to the shelves or closets, no questions asked. Other times, 617 North West Street was as a light house radiating help to many when their 'sea was too wide and their boat was too small.'

When La Rita picked us up at the airport she did not take us to our vacant house. No, she took us to her already full house. She and Jim had found us a place to rent on their street. My possessions had been deposited there by a moving company, but it would probably be a month before there was any time or energy to unpack boxes and to move in.

You and Audrey were sleeping soundly, what with the long trip and the late hour. I felt that I needed to be alone and have some personal moments to consider our lives in the past and to try to imagine what lay ahead. I slipped out of the Couch house around three a.m. and hobbled in the direction of the community park, where I found a substantial bench that could bear the weight of my piteous situation. I needed to cry in solitude, but instead I heard an authoritative voice saying, "What are you doing?" "I am sitting on this bench, officer," I replied. "Why?" he pressed. "Well, I have huge problems and I am crying here." I thought he'd leave me alone, but he was protecting the citizens and the property of Cordell, Oklahoma. He told me to "go home." I answered that, "I don't have a home." It was useless. He followed in the police cruiser as I hobbled back to the Couch habitat for humanity. "Revolting," I thought, "and here I am in bedroom slippers because I twisted my ankle in some airport." I was mortified that the policeman escorted me to the front door and woke up Jim and La Rita to see if they wanted me inside. (Jim looked like he wasn't sure.)

That night as you slept, I forced myself to lie awake and fill my mind with some positive thoughts. I had a talk with myself about the full life that you enjoyed in spite of the relentless illness. You had been privileged to be granted two miraculous remissions. And, I mused that you had sampled many pleasures in your ten year span. You and Audrey were acquainted with some wonderful choices of entertainment: I was thinking of "Fiddler on the Roof," "1776" and "Disney on Parade." We mustn't omit William Shakespeare.

One memorable night comes vividly into focus as I recall a darkened living room scene illuminated with multiple candles. I had tried to tell the story of *Romeo and Juliet* to you and Audrey. With apologies to William, you girls were not too moved. Undaunted, I played the entire soundtrack from an excellent film production, and insisted on absolute silence and attention to it. The play ends with "All are punished... The sun for sorrow will not show his head... For never was a story of more woe than this of Juliet and her Romeo." Well, dear heart, seldom did a performance have such a captivated and responsive audience. We all sobbed, then laughed at ourselves. I felt victorious that I could expose you to such heavy material which you understood so well.

Now with this mental picture of golden recollection, I attempted to join you in peaceful slumber. Other lines from the work which were burned into my memory came forward to take a bow. I heard them as revolving prayers in my head: "Parting is such sweet sorrow that I shall say good night till it be morrow. Good night, good night! As sweet repose and rest come to thy heart as that within my breast! Sweet good night! A thousand times good night! Night's candles are burnt out...'*

---

* Romeo and Juliet, William Shakespeare

Chapter 14: Yellow Roses

On demerol by injection, you put on an admirable front. Doctor Couch was sending his nurses from his outpatient office to his home in order to administer the pain killer when we called for help. The policy wasn't satisfactory for very long because your anguish was increasing, and sometimes we'd have to wait while the nurses attended to duties at the office. It was agony for you to lie down, so you remained in a seated position, dozing when hurts mercifully released their grip on you. You still smiled and tried to read or watch television, and mostly you'd tell me, "I'm fine." I found myself wanting to protect you, even to speak for you. But, just prior to entering Cordell Memorial Hospital, you made a request to ride one of the Couch twins' ten speed bikes around the block. Doctor Couch honored your request. I could hardly watch this demonstration of sheer bravado. It was so like, when as tiny children, you and Audrey would perform dangerous feats on your playground gear that would chill me to the very bone. I adopted the philosophy then, that if I didn't look, nothing would happen. Time hadn't changed the magic!

Cordell Memorial Hospital was to be our headquarters jointly. The policy of an adult "rooming in" with a child had been in effect for years before we made ourselves known there. We enormously appreciated that policy. To my relief, it was decided to continue some treatment as long as your blood and your general condition would permit. You were not hospitalized solely for comfort. We were all in there pitching, and praying that vincristine would once again conquer some evils. No one suggested palliative or supportive measures to either one of us. In addition to periwinkle juice, the doctor prescribed an oral steroid, prednisone, which kept you free of fever, and somewhat euphoric.

I can say that we discovered a unique sort of happiness for at least the first ten days of "our" confinements? Both of us read a good bit of light, funny material. I purchased a small chalkboard, which we used as a daily bulletin directed at outsiders. From your window, visitors read varied messages like: "LET US OUT, WARDEN," "ONE B.L.T. ON THE DOUBLE," or a simple one word plea . . . "HELP!" We used the latter bulletin over and over, because of the response that it often brought. How many times, do you suppose, Good Samaritans came to the door of your room to ask how they might render assistance?

Then, there was a one word increase to our vocabularies, catawampus. As the doctor was making his morning rounds, or perhaps it was afternoon, he said, "Goll-lee, Mommy must really have been tired, 'cause when I peeked in today she was sleeping all catawampus." That word fell on blushing ears, and I made a very speedy and sincere apology. Memorial is a Baptist-sponsored hospital, and there was I all catawampus for the world to see! Neither of us could venture a guess as to WHAT was exposed to WHOM??? I have since learned that the word means only to be askew or cater-cornered.

The laboratory staff had a doll made for you. It was adorable, and it was just right for you. The doll, reminiscent of Raggedy Ann, had two faces . . . a sleeping countenance and a wide-awake smiling one. The doll slept when you did, and joyfully received visitors when you did. Visitors and staff learned to check the doll's face as a signal to come in or to stay out. One of the nurses must have measured your feet while both of us napped . . . anonymously, she gifted you with hand made slippers that perfectly fit and warmed your swollen feet. I had looked unsuccessfully for days in all the shops to find something to fit and unfreeze your poor feet, which didn't look like feet anymore. This kind soul (I'll never know who she was) fashioned crochet booties for you which were shaped like kitchen canister lids. They were green, and you never took them off. It was beautifully evident how much everyone who surrounded you genuinely cared for you. They showed you three newborn babies. You welcomed them directly after their parents said hello. You were special, really special!

Audrey was your most revered visitor by a country mile. She came to call on you whenever you asked for her. You never wanted her around to see you suffer. Once she came at 10:30 p.m. because that was when all conditions were favorable. You missed your sister, and you were relatively free of pain then. Audrey and I could ruin your day or evening if we let our sorrow and compassion be recognizable to you. What a dignified person, my Tracy, you were above having people cry over your adversity.

I want to thank you for showing me such regard when you were sick. I am so grateful that you took such fine care of me. Yes, I stated that correctly. The night nurse told me how it happened that I could enjoy juice and coffee with you each morning. You instructed her to order those choices for the breakfast tray, along with the usual apple juice and chocolate shake, your own particular fare. Dr. Couch said he wouldn't put in an intravenous if you ate and drank a little something every day. The menu choices were yours. Upon occasion you fancied ice cream or a corn dog from the Dairy Freeze. Another favorite was a simple bowl of cooked asparagus, which you ordered often. Dr. Jim would ask, "Is that you stinkin' up my hospital with that mushy asparagus?" That made you laugh. I think you ordered the dish so frequently just to get his reaction. Mornings never were my best hours. I was born sleepy and every morning is like a new birth to me . . . new, as in traumatic! Well, my daughter didn't let me down on this score, either. Each nurse who entered your room, when the dawn came up like thunder, was briefed by you in a whisper to keep the overhead lights off and to go about her duties silently, out of

75

consideration for your mother. One morning I awakened certain that I was hallucinating. The first sight my eyes fell upon was that of my daughter standing on a chair, clothes hanger in hand, to pull down a change of underwear. You had always been extremely independent, but this was ridiculous, particularly since the pain you were experiencing called for morphine. (known as "sulfate" to you) When asked why you would do such a dangerous thing, you sweetly admitted that you saw no reason to disturb my rest.

One morning a dozen spectacular roses were delivered to you. They were yellow and fragrant and they were a gift from your Dad. Instead of being surprised and delighted, your reaction was out of character for you. You became very angry and agitated and you told me to throw them away. I responded that I certainly would not throw away anything so beautiful, and that your Dad really wanted you to have them. You pointed to the waste basket and insisted that I throw them away. It was clear that you didn't want those flowers. Abruptly, you switched gears and told me that a baby had been born a few hours ago. You said, "Take them to the mommy. Who knows, maybe she'll name the baby after me." It was an order from you that I felt I couldn't ignore. Thus, a new mommy at Cordell Memorial received a gift from a little girl she did not know. You must have been very frustrated that your father chose not to be with you during those very difficult days. The gesture he made was not enough. I also think you had a glimpse into your immortality that morning, and that you made a loving gesture to a stranger who might just name her newborn, Tracy. I never learned the outcome, but no matter.

Dr. Jim entered your room another morning to find you in tears. That was such an unusual situation for you and, of course, he thought you likely had a lot of pain. Yes, but this was pain of an emotional type. You missed Frizzle, and how do we allow dogs into the hospital domain? Dr. Couch inquired of me when you might feel the best during a given day. I guessed that would be late in the day close to dinner. Then he was gone. The next day your doctor swooped into your room and without a word, lifted you out of bed, sheets trailing down the hall, and carefully put you inside his orange pumpkin of a station wagon. I had to really step lively to keep up with you. There was a four-legged passenger inside to greet you and to take a little ride around town with you. The dog seemed positively human. I admonished her to behave and to not jump all over you. Not an ounce of her pressed against your poor lower abdomen. You rode like two love birds, heads together, sighing endearing phrases to one another. I overheard you say to Frizzle, "I don't know if I'll ever see you again . . . this time I think I'm sick enough to die." I prodded to ask what you said to your wire haired buddy. Your answer: "Oh, nothing." You never let me in on your secret. Thanks for sparing me the worst. Once inside the hospital I thought that Prince Charming had surely granted you your wish. It was no mistake coming back to Oklahoma.

I could elaborate on the individual miseries that were yours during the next week or more. However, I prefer to keep as much dignity in this record of your life as is possible. Let it suffice to say that you grew silent as the mute cygnet swan, except to urgently call out for another shot to assuage the torment for a couple of hours. This pelvic mass caused extreme pressure, making you feel like you needed to use the bathroom endlessly. I can only guess that the pressure was very much like fruitless labor pain.

Your sister was not granted permission to visit with you anymore... She made frequent trips outside your window, sometimes bringing Frizzle with her... In this way your contact with those you loved was never completely stopped... It delighted me to know how much those sixty-second waves and smiles meant to you both. When the laboratory reported that your blood picture was poor, too poor to have another course of vincristine, I looked at you more objectively than ever before... what I saw terrorized me. This child, whom I adored, was deteriorating in every physical sense. Your body's descent was fast, so fiercely abrupt.

Audrey was brought to me in the doctors' lounge for a private conversation. Mine was the tongue that uttered unbelievable words for her to try to grasp. Our little "sunshine" was unable to hold back the torrent of rain, as I explained that it was nearly inevitable that our loss might be heaven's gain. I told her not to lose faith, not to give up . . . but at the same time to trust that our Lord would care for her sister better than we should she not recover this time.

Do you recall asking Doctor Jim if he considered surgery in your case? It was out of the realm of reason, but I commend you on your spirit. You were down, but not defeated! "Just how many problems do I have?" You asked this without batting a blue eye. He very honestly estimated five distinct, big problems. "Then, why don't you operate and take out two?" He assured you that he would confer with some of the specialists at Presbyterian. All of us knew that this was a pipe dream never to materialize. The last word was left up to you . . . did you want to travel two hours east for the proper evaluation? No, you decided that you wanted to remain in the room that had become so familiar, and in the care of the doctor with the giant shoes, who gave, with no extra charge, special "head-kisses" at the close of each day.

We borrowed a prayer from St. Thomas More to say together often during our confinements. "Pray for me as I will for thee, that we may merrily meet in heaven." When you had gone to sleep as comfortably as the lounge chair could cradle you, I did much soul-searching, usually by reading something inspirational. Marion Craig wrote, "I do not ask that I should ever stand among the wise, the worthy, or the great; I only ask that softly, hand in hand, a child and I may enter at Thy gate."

Our very "human" wire haired fox terrier

Chapter 15: Rocking Back Somewhere

July twenty-eighth is here. This day revealed a frustrated, agonized, exhausted little girl. You were cold and nervous; your hurts simply refused to be relieved. Your anxiety was a condition I had never before witnessed. This intense pain persisted seven hours. Suddenly you pleaded for help as your chest began to ache, and you were gasping for oxygen. Tracy, I felt wholly bewildered and helpless. That is why I cautiously chose to position myself near, but behind you. I didn't want you to see me sad and dejected beyond the point where I could give anything but my presence. Even then you were aware of what I needed. You asked your mommy to sit very close to you so that I could rub your arms and legs that felt so stiff and numb. Oh, thank God I was permitted to do something for you! You told me softly that you loved me . . . . After awhile a huge smile lit your face . . . You said you felt like you were in motion, rocking back. I misunderstood and thought you were describing a fainting sensation. "No, Mommy, it's fun, like rocking on a ride back somewhere." There followed another unforgettable smile, then Doctor Couch said, "She's gone, Pat. It's all over." I don't remember weeping, dear, only sitting there dazed and trembling for too long. Of this I am sure; you were absent from that room. The spirit which was yours was already present with the Lord. I was aware of LaRita and many others tenderly touching me, and of the sounds of stifled sobbing behind me. I heard myself addressing Doctor Couch with "Please, please hold me." He had to give up someone very dear, too. It was not God's plan for you to die . . . but when it happened, He had a room reserved for you. I felt very strongly about this, and it was the chief reason why I didn't lie down and die with you.

A song that held a fascination for me years ago comes to mind when I recall your silent last week on earth. The lyrics ring true to your story: "The silver swan who, living, had no note, when death approach'd unlock'd her silent throat. Leaning her breast against the reedy shore, Thus sang her first and last and sang no more: Farewell, all joys! O death, come, close mine eyes; More geese than swans now live, more fools than wise."*

A little while after you passed into the perfect life, the funeral director came to introduce himself to me. At once, I became defensive and protective and close to rude. I stood, so that we'd be certain to have the important direct eye level with each other. My shaky, destroyed voice was dismissed, and I summoned up an authoritative command ordering him to be gentle, VERY gentle, with my daughter. I went on to say that he would be touching and lifting precious cargo, and that he was to treat that cargo with the utmost respect. And above all, I repeated, "BE GENTLE WITH HER!"

Your funeral services were handled in just the way that was acceptable to me. (And, I trust, to you.) I attempted to give the impression that the occasion was one of promotion or advancement. You were dressed in a green skirt and white ruffled blouse. Your only accessory was a schnauzer pin, a gift from Aunt Kay. You looked then, as if you might have been clad for the first day in the fifth grade. Inside the church, the message and the music bound together to clearly show your youthful uninhibited love of God... I had only to bring to mind those two last smiles you showed to me to prod myself into the realization that a victory had been won. You had slayed every dragon along life's way.

---

* The Silver Swan, words by Christopher Hatton

For Audrey and me, the penetrating sorrow remained. We all anticipate that the old will precede the young in death. If there is a more stabbing kind of grief than to give up a child, I can't imagine it!

As I recall, Audrey and I began moving into the brick rental house about three weeks after you died. You had never seen the house that we hoped to make our home, so I guess it was understandable that I tried to show it to you on some level. I wanted very much for you to be able to see the pretty bedroom I had planned for you. A rose colored chenille bedspread topped your pretty bed. Resting on the pillow was your waking-sleeping doll from the hospital and other favorites that you had accumulated. I arranged your closet and drawers, and even had your shoes lined up on the closet floor. I didn't intend a shrine, but I just wanted you to "see" it for a while, and it was all too soon to give away your possessions. When Audrey was in school, I used to lie down on your bed and try to be with you. I wanted to sense the peace that I thought you had now.

My awful nightmares began soon after we moved in. I would drift off to sleep okay, but then it began: There was a knock on my front door. It was you. You were so happy, so divinely happy, to visit your sister and me. You looked healthy and vivacious as you played physically with Audrey. You demonstrated cartwheels and jumping jacks and laughed heartily. I was in the kitchen or in the bathroom fussing and fidgeting. I was putting on a little makeup and adjusting my gold choker necklace with the large black stone. I was clearly wearing the black knit dress that I wore to your funeral. You began to implore me with, "Look at me, look at me, I'm alive." I told you softly that "I know you think you are alive, but you died, and tomorrow we are going to have services for you." You protested over and over to tell me that you are not dead but very much alive. Now I literally began to wring my hands and cry. "No, Tracy, we will have a funeral for you where we'll sing songs and hear messages about you. You really are dead and tomorrow you will have to lie down in the damned box!" I woke myself at this intolerable place. I could do it if I didn't take the sleeping aid Dr. Couch prescribed. This dream went on night after horrible night, and I asked Jim to help me. No expert on dreams, he set up an appointment with Pastor Laddie, who had studied dreams only recently.

I fairly dragged myself into the pastor's study looking just as I was, overwrought with grief and sleep deprivation. I told Laddie that I was terribly conflicted. I was so sad that you were no longer here with us, but at the same time genuinely "spooked" that you came to me every night in the form of a dream. Laddie was not spooked or even puzzled. At first I was a trifle annoyed that he was so casually confident. He listened intently, to be sure, but his little smile was growing bigger and his icy blue eyes fairly danced. His chair was leaning back casually on two legs, and his pipe smoke circled playfully. (Santa Claus kept coming to my tired brain.)

Laddie finally spoke, saying, "I got to know your Tracy pretty well in the hospital . . . And if I am correct, she will come to you as often as she has to, until you believe that she is not dead." He reiterated that he was absolutely sure that you were determined enough to knock on my door as many nights as it took for you to show me that you were very much alive.

Just a few evenings later I got a phone call from Texas. It was our dear hair stylist, Estelle. She had wanted so much to visit you in Cordell Memorial during your last days there. You were no longer receiving visitors because you "thought you looked and acted like a moron!" It was the morphine, of course, but you didn't want people, whom you loved, to see you that way. It was not debatable. Estelle and her husband had retired from the military and moved on to her home state. She jumped right in saying, "I know about Tracy." "Oh, Estelle," I answered, "I didn't know that her obituary was carried in Texas." "No obituary, my friend, your daughter came to me in my dream." Your former beautician said that you were clearly running joyously and free in a pastoral setting, "Look at me now, look at my hair, Estelle!" Our kind friend had called to tell me that you were indeed alive, ecstatically happy and modeling a glowing head of hair. The lesson: I had to stop telling you and myself that you were dead. I had to be still and listen to my daughter bearing witness that she was most assuredly alive. No more nightmares, no more nightmares.

The Christmas season is upon the world as these words are being written. This week, as we trimmed the tree, sadly half the ornaments had been labeled yours. When the job was finished, both of us experienced a sinking spell that didn't want to loose its grip on us. Your sister and I broke the dike of tears we had been holding back. Right then I decided that this Christmas could be the worst or the best we'd ever observed. You must remember the birthday cakes for Jesus you and Audrey so painstakingly decorated year after year. Well, this year will be no different at our house. Our mortal joy will not equal the celestial joy that you will experience, but we are going to try to feel some of that ecstatic rapture through the communion with saints, such as you. "Help us, darling," I asked. And, help us, you did.

It has been our custom to read aloud the familiar Christmas story as recorded by Luke, the Physician, usually on Christmas eve. I reached up on the shelf for your children's bible, and a loose page spiraled down softly to my hands like a snowflake. My whole body was brought to a stop as I recognized your handwriting. They were the last words you'd ever written in your own distinctive script. It had been written the day we were in the exhaustive stages of moving to Oklahoma. You wrote, "Ecclesiastes Chapter 3 To everything there is a season a time to be born and a time to die." You had not finished the verses or even inserted punctuation, but you provided the message. Heaven came down that December to herald God's perfect order in His wondrous universe.

Allow me a tiny postscript, please. Your sister speaks of you every day. Recently she tried to conjure the heavenly vision that you are now. She thinks you have long, thick hair, a body with no scars or "zippers," and, while all the other cherubs and celestial beings are dressed in white . . she just KNOWS you are the one in purple, because that's your favorite color. We will be so eager to join you one of these days to see how well the description fits!

Tracy age 9, Ocean City, NJ.
A tough soldier in a red bikini.

Epilogue

Music, poetry and the creative arts are supposed to touch the heart. And, so they do, in my instance. On the countless four hundred mile round trip runs to and from Buffalo, the radio served as the third presence in our little Volkswagen. One tune held special significance for both of us. You liked it, as I did, however, I was unable to sing it or even hear it without a restricting lump in my throat. When it played I was relieved that you rested in the back seat unable to see my silent, spontaneous release of tears. The song was Frank Sinatra's rendition of, "MY WAY."* It seems to have been inspired as a duet for the both of us. It goes exactly like this:

Tracy: And now the end is near, and so I face the final curtain,

My friend, I'll say it clear, I'll state my case, of which I'm certain.

I've lived a life that's full, I traveled each and every highway,

And more, much more than this, I did it My Way.

Mommy: Regrets, I've had a few, but then again, too few to mention,

I did what I had to do, and saw it thru without exemption.

---

* My Way written by Paul Anka

89

I planned each chartered course, each careful step along the by-way,

And more, much more than this, I did it My Way.

Tracy: Yes, there were times, I'm sure you knew,

when I bit off more than I could chew,

But thru it all, when there was doubt, I ate it up, and spit it out.

I faced it all, and I stood tall, and did it My Way.

Mommy: I've loved, I've laughed I've cried, I've had my fill, my share of losing...

To think I did all that, and may I say, "Not in a shy way."

Oh, no, oh no, not me, I did it My Way...

Together: The record shows, (we) took the blows, and did it (Our) Way.*

You were unique. You were a tough soldier in a red bikini. You seldom questioned the tragic falls that earmarked the many corners of your years, simply because you saw and partook of so many more pleasures. I will never forget the lyrical laughter which was yours. As well, when I say your name I say it with no faltering hesitation. A great injustice would be done if you were quietly, reverently thought of as that unfortunate sick child who didn't make it. I pray that everyone will reach the sensible conclusion that you DID MAKE IT. You made your life count with zest that was appealing and marvelous. One day I will be able to rejoice in the fullest measure that my darling is, and ever was, a saint . . . A CHILD OF THE KING! Five words in closing my part of your adventure must be, Amen and so be it!

As lovingly remembered by your Mommy

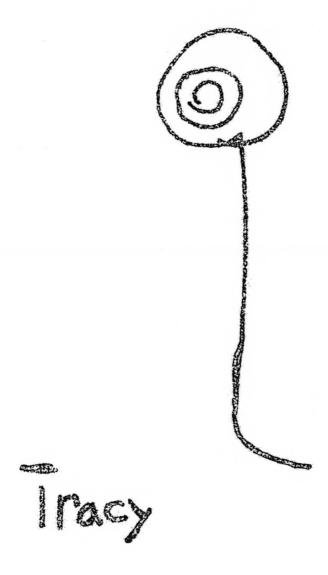

*taking herself to a higher place and starting again**

* Tracy's drawing interpreted by Bernie Siegel, M.D.

About the Author

Patricia Klinger Schrope lives with her husband, Eugene, in a 112 year old house surrounded by the Blue Mountains in central Pennsylvania. She can unpack now, but prior to residing here Patricia has lived in more than fifteen homes in seven states.

A graduate of the University of Pennsylvania, English and Writing were always her favorite subjects. She has done freelance writing for several newspapers. The gift of a computer a couple of years ago, when she didn't even know how to turn the mechanical device on, turned out to make all things possible.

Patricia's passion is her small, loving family. It doesn't get any better than to experience the beach, music, theatre and movies with her close kindred circle. That circle surely includes Trilby, the latest wacky wire haired fox terrier, who shares the author's life and bed.

"Patricia Schrope's deeply reflective thinking is tonic for all parents, but it should particularly prompt some soul-searching for those currently raising young children."

----John Troutman
    Editorial writer and editorial board member
    The Patriot-News, Harrisburg, PA

Breinigsville, PA USA
29 October 2009
226698BV00001B/100/A